D1613778

THE DAKOTA ACCESS PIPELINE

BY SUE BRADFORD EDWARDS

CONTENT CONSULTANT

CLIFFORD VILLA
ASSISTANT PROFESSOR OF LAW
UNIVERSITY OF NEW MEXICO

Essential Library

An Imprint of Abdo Publishing | abdopublishing.com

abdopublishing.com

Published by Abdo Publishing, a division of ABDO, PO Box 398166, Minneapolis,
Minnesota 55439. Copyright © 2018 by Abdo Consulting Group, Inc. International
copyrights reserved in all countries. No part of this book may be reproduced in
any form without written permission from the publisher. Essential Library™ is a
trademark and logo of Abdo Publishing.

Printed in the United States of America, North Mankato, Minnesota
092017
012018

**THIS BOOK CONTAINS
RECYCLED MATERIALS**

Cover Photo: Terray Sylvester/VWPics/AP Images
Interior Photos: Terray Sylvester/VWPics/AP Images, 4–5, 10, 17, 48, 81, 85; Andrew
Cullen/Reuters/Newscom, 13; Tom Stromme/The Bismarck Tribune/AP Images, 18–19;
Red Line Editorial, 21; Martha Irvine/AP Images, 25; Karl Bodmer/Travels in the
Interior of North America, 28–29; Universal History Archive/Universal Images Group/
Getty Images, 38; Library of Congress, 41; James MacPherson/AP Images, 42–43;
Erik McGregor/Sipa USA/AP Images, 51; Hulton Archive/Getty Images, 52–53; Chet
Brokaw/AP Images, 57; Tyler Bell/AP Images, 65; Steve Oehlenschlager/iStockphoto,
66–67; iStockphoto, 71; US Energy Information Administration, 76; Jacquelyn Martin/
AP Images, 78–79; Darryl Dyck/The Canadian Press/AP Images, 89; Rex Features/AP
Images, 90–91; Al Hartmann/The Salt Lake Tribune/AP Images, 94; David Goldman/
AP Images, 99

Editor: Melissa York
Series Designer: Maggie Villaume

Publisher's Cataloging-in-Publication Data

Names: Edwards, Sue Bradford, author.
Title: The Dakota Access Pipeline / by Sue Bradford Edwards.
Description: Minneapolis, Minnesota : Abdo Publishing, 2018. | Series: Special reports
    | Includes bibliographic references and index.
Identifiers: LCCN 2017946877 | ISBN 9781532113321 (lib.bdg.) | ISBN 9781532152207
    (ebook)
Subjects: LCSH: Public utilities--Juvenile literature. | North Dakota--Juvenile
    literature. | Gas pipelines--Juvenile literature. | Dissenting opinions--
    Juvenile literature.
Classification: DDC 388.5--dc23
LC record available at https://lccn.loc.gov/2017946877

CONTENTS

Chapter One
YOUTH LEADING THE WAY   4

Chapter Two
BUILDING DAPL   18

Chapter Three
RESERVATION LANDS   28

Chapter Four
INDIGENOUS RIGHTS   42

Chapter Five
WATER SAFETY   52

Chapter Six
THE PRICE OF OIL   66

Chapter Seven
NO SINGLE PLAN   78

Chapter Eight
DAPL AND THE FUTURE   90

Essential Facts   100   Source Notes   106
Glossary   102   Index   110
Additional Resources   104   About the Author   112

CHAPTER ONE

YOUTH LEADING
THE WAY

As the Rezpect Our Water video opens, a girl steps into view and introduces herself: "My name is Tokata Iron Eyes. I'm 12 years old. I live in Fort Yates, North Dakota." The scene transitions to another girl, who introduces herself as 16-year-old Anastasia White Mountain. Following the introductions, various young speakers from the Standing Rock Reservation reveal to viewers that they are Native American. Then they go on to discuss activities they enjoy. "I often go to the river. I love to swim," says Iron Eyes.

"Running off the boat docks with each other and jumping off at the same time," says 14-year-old Wynona Gayton.

Teens and children got involved in the protest movement to stop the construction of the Dakota Access Pipeline.

"Down to the river to swim or we sit there and talk," said an anonymous teen boy.

Off camera, an interviewer asks them what they think of the Dakota Access Pipeline (DAPL) that would soon cross the Missouri River, close to where reservation residents get their drinking water. "It's really messed up is what it is," said Gayton, "'cause we get all our water from the Missouri River."[1]

REZPECT OUR WATER

The video is one of four that Standing Rock youth made as part of the Rezpect Our Water media campaign, posted in March and April 2016. They agreed to help make the videos after speakers visited their school and told students about the plan to finish building DAPL near the reservation. The Standing Rock Reservation is home to people from the Lakota and Dakota Nations, who are known by many outsiders as the Sioux.

DAPL is not just of interest to the reservation. It is a part of the infrastructure used to move fuel across the United States. The pipeline was designed and built by Energy Transfer Partners (ETP) to carry crude oil from the Bakken oil fields in North Dakota to distant shipping points in Illinois. In early planning stages, the proposed route for the pipeline passed just north of Bismarck, North Dakota's capitol, but residents of the city objected that the pipeline passed too close to areas that supplied their water. The pipeline was shifted south of Bismarck to a point just 0.5 miles (0.8 km) upstream from the Standing Rock Reservation. Because the new route would cross the Missouri River at Lake Oahe, this small portion of the pipeline and the land easement required to build it needed to be approved by the US Army Corps of Engineers (USACE).

The people of the reservation were told the pipeline, buried underground, would be no threat to their

USACE: WHO ARE THEY AND WHAT DO THEY DO?

The United States Army Corps of Engineers (USACE) is the world's largest public engineering organization. The group employs more than 35,000 civilian engineers, and it is responsible for environmental cleanup on lands controlled by the Department of Defense, such as military bases and testing facilities. It also oversees the development of wetlands and water-related projects carried out in relation to the Clean Water Act of 1972, which legally limits water pollution.

One reason the USACE is involved in the DAPL project is the pipeline route crosses federal lands controlled by the US Army. In addition to Lake Oahe in North and South Dakota, these include Lake Sakakawea in North Dakota and Carlyle Reservoir in Illinois. The USACE has jurisdiction over only the parts of the pipeline that cross these specific areas.

drinking water, but Tokata and other students disagreed with this assessment. They knew that people and animals that drink oil or oil-tainted water get sick. An oil spill could permanently damage the area, much as it had done when the ship *Exxon Valdez* struck a reef off Alaska and dumped 11 million gallons (41.6 million L) of oil into the sea in 1989.[2] The students wanted to protect the earth, so they agreed to help make videos with the Rezpect Our Water campaign. In the video, reservation residents as young as six discuss their concerns about this pipeline and their frustration that they seemed to matter less than the residents of Bismarck. "They aren't the ones being affected," said Tokata about the new route, "so why should they get to make the decision?" But the students weren't willing to give up without trying to do something to stop what they see as injustice. "We may be small," said Anastasia, "but together we have a big voice."[3]

PROTECTORS, PROTESTERS, AND VIOLENCE

As much as the people of Standing Rock hoped the students' videos would help convince people that the pipeline should not be completed, they knew they had to do more. Clean water was at stake, along with historic sites and sacred lands, including burial grounds threatened by the pipeline construction. These burials include family members of protesters like Ladonna Allard Brave Bull, whose father and son are both buried in the area. On April 1, 2016, Brave Bull set up an encampment, called Sacred Circle, on her own land near Cannon Ball, North Dakota. Located near the confluence of the Cannon Ball and Missouri Rivers, this was a camp for prayer.

"THIS DEMOLITION IS DEVASTATING. THESE GROUNDS ARE THE RESTING PLACES OF OUR ANCESTORS. THE ANCIENT CAIRNS AND STONE PRAYER RINGS THERE CANNOT BE REPLACED. IN ONE DAY, OUR SACRED LAND HAS BEEN TURNED INTO HOLLOW GROUND."[4]

—DAVID ARCHAMBAULT II, STANDING ROCK TRIBAL CHAIR

At first, those in the camps were mostly local people, but as word of the protest grew, more and more supporters from around the world arrived. Many people of this resistance movement came to call themselves water protectors. A second camp was set up in August. It was named *Oceti Sakowin,* or Seven Council Fires, and Tokata visited this camp whenever she was able. She described her visits:

Because I was on summer vacation, every day I'd go to the Oceti

Sakowin camp to take part in the peaceful protest. It was a

happy place. People from around the country traveled to join

us, and we shared stories and learned from each other. . . . There

were thousands of us. It was powerful to see so many people

coming together.[5]

Many of those who gathered in the camps participated in peaceful protests, but as thousands of people poured into the camps, a number of the protests became violent. People burned cars and stacked logs across the road and set the wood on fire. A reporter heard another protester pleading with one of the violent groups. "Stop lighting these barricades on fire, brothers! I'm a member of the Standing Rock Sioux tribe," he said. "After this, I have to live here."[6]

OCETI SAKOWIN

Oceti Sakowin means Seven Council Fires. Originally the Sioux were made up of seven large related groups of people, each with its own council fire around which the group would gather as a community. The fire also symbolizes continuity because as the people moved their camps from place to place, they would take a coal from the old fire and use it to light a new fire in the new location.

Images in the media showed police in riot gear driving up in armored personnel carriers in a scene that looked more like a

Water protectors display signs from dugout canoes near the Oceti Sakowin camp.

military campaign than law enforcement. On September 3, a private security company turned dogs loose on the protesters. On November 20, when protesters refused to clear the highway, the authorities brought in hoses on fire trucks and soaked people with water despite the freezing weather. "The irony!" said Tokata, reacting to the fact that the protesters were trying to protect water and water was being used against them.[7]

TAKING SIDES

On December 4, 2016, the USACE announced that it was denying the final permit ETP needed to complete the segment of the pipeline near Standing Rock Reservation, based upon the need for further information and analysis of alternatives. As stated by Jo-Ellen Darcy, the army's

DOG ATTACKS

On September 3, 2016, a group of unarmed, chanting protesters positioned themselves between the machinery needed to finish laying the pipeline and the pipeline itself and refused to move. The security company hired to disperse them approached with pepper spray and dogs, unleashing the animals and setting them on the protesters. Following the attacks, a woman pulled aside her shirt and showed the injury she received to a reporter. "I stood there unarmed yelling at them and they smugly looked at us and they smiled every time the dog lunged at us," she told reporters.[8] Activists transmitted photos of these attacks around social media, making comparisons to the use of dogs against civil rights protesters in Selma, Alabama, in the 1960s.

assistant secretary for civil works, "The best way to complete that work responsibly and expeditiously is to explore alternate routes for the pipeline crossing."[9]

Tokata and other water protectors celebrated the victory that this halt represented, but they also realized the fight wasn't over. "This movement isn't just about our reservation—it's about speaking up when you feel that something is wrong," said Tokata.[10] This was a fight that

Located on the banks of the Cannon Ball River, the Oceti Sakowin camp filled with tents, tepees, and campers.

the Lakota had been fighting for generations, and, win or lose, they didn't expect it to end here.

After all, not everyone who spoke out supported the water protectors. Many people were vocal about wanting the pipeline to be finished because ETP promised to hire workers and there would be tax money for the state of North Dakota. Supporters also believe the pipeline is a quicker, safer, more affordable way to transport oil, compared to transportation by railway. Using the pipeline would, according to supporters, help the United States be less dependent on foreign oil. To understand how a pipeline could matter so much to different groups of people all over the United States, it is essential to understand Native American history, the role of water and energy in the environment, and the pipeline itself.

MORE TO THE
STORY

WHO IS PROFITING FROM DAPL?

Some critics of the Standing Rock protesters, like Naomi Schaefer Riley, a columnist for the *New York Post*, believe the people from the reservation who don't want the pipeline are making bad economic decisions. "In one of the counties where the Standing Rock Sioux live, the high school graduation rate is only 14 percent. So some of this is clearly just the story of a people with no resources or ideas on how to bring resources to their communities."[11] Although the residents of the reservation were asking for a clean river, not money, Riley told an interviewer from the *Pipeline and Gas Journal*, "I think that if the company had offered the tribe a sufficient lump sum payment, the project would have been successful."[12]

On the other side, there are four companies investing in the pipeline, which means they are expecting to make money from its operation. They have all borrowed heavily to fund the construction. Energy Transfer Partners borrowed $3.75 billion, Sunoco Logistics $2.5 billion, Dakota Access $2.5 billion, and Energy Transfer Equity $1.5 billion.[13] These companies counted on earnings from the pipeline to pay back these loans and also to profit. If oil does not flow through the pipeline regularly and on time, they could be in financial trouble.

FROM THE
HEADLINES

WEAPONIZED WATER

Media reported that on November 20–21, 2016, police used tear gas, rubber bullets, and water cannons against some of the Standing Rock protesters. Morton County Sheriff Kyle Kirchmeier said water cannons were not brought in and only fire hoses were used. Sheriff's spokesperson Rob Keller explained that a tactical vehicle spraying tear gas was mistaken by some people as a water cannon. Although a fire hose is normally considered a nonlethal option, the temperatures in the area reached -18 degrees Fahrenheit (-27.8°C) overnight. Linda Black Elk, a Standing Rock resident and member of the Medic and Healer Council, reported that as temperatures dropped, people's clothing froze, sometimes to their bodies, and the frozen clothing crackled as they walked. In a letter from US executive director Margaret Huang, the human rights organization Amnesty International warned the sheriff's office to stop using hoses before someone died of hypothermia. Hypothermia occurs when the body loses heat faster than it can produce it. It can be caused by immersion in cold water or exposure to cold weather, can affect the heart, memory, and coordination, and can even be fatal. Although no one died immediately after being sprayed, 300 people were treated for their injuries, and 26 were hospitalized.[14]

Frigid temperatures gripped the camp
in November.

BUILDING
DAPL

A pipeline is a long pipe that carries oil, natural gas, or another fluid over a great distance. Most often pipelines are buried underground, so many Americans are unaware of the miles of pipelines that run across the United States.

The Dakota Access Pipeline is 1,172 miles (1,886 km) long and 30 inches (76 cm) in diameter.[1] It runs from the Bakken oil fields in North Dakota to Patoka, Illinois. DAPL carries the oil from where it was extracted from the ground to shipping points so that it can be transported to refineries, where it will be turned into gasoline, diesel fuel, and other petroleum products. The pipeline's builder, ETP, specializes in pipeline construction.

Construction equipment buries a section of DAPL.

BAKKEN CRUDE

The oil that DAPL carries, Bakken crude, comes from the Bakken formation, one of the largest deposits of oil and natural gas in the United States. This geologic formation stretches beneath large areas of northwestern North Dakota and northeastern Montana, up into the Canadian provinces of Saskatchewan and Manitoba. The rock formation itself is composed of a layer of shale topped by a layer of sandstone, with another layer of shale on top of that. All three layers of stone contain oil and natural gas.

Although this formation contains oil, the oil is not easy to remove because the various stones have a low permeability. This means the oil does not flow easily through the stone. Because of this low flow, the well has to have a longer drill hole, called a bore or a shaft, through the pay zone, the rock

MILES AND MILES

The United States has the most extensive pipeline system in the world, with more than 2.4 million miles (3.8 million km) of pipeline crisscrossing the nation. These pipelines range in size from small-diameter natural gas pipelines that deliver fuel to people's homes to large pipelines like DAPL that deliver crude oil to distribution points. Approximately 72,000 miles (116,000 km) of pipeline carry crude oil.[2] Other pipelines carry refined oil products such as gasoline, heating oil, diesel fuel, aviation gasoline, jet fuel, and kerosene.

DAPL runs through four states.

with recoverable oil. Because the oil-bearing bodies of rock in the Bakken field are shallow but wide—a shape called a lens—the oil shafts must be drilled horizontally to exploit the pay zone. This was not possible until a new drilling method, fracking, was perfected and came into widespread use in the 2000s.

Fracking is short for "hydraulic fracturing." It is a method used to drill for petroleum, a general term for crude oil and natural gas. In fracking, a vertical shaft is drilled down from the surface, leading to a horizontal shaft that extends into the oil deposit. Water, sand, and chemicals are blasted down this shaft and into the rock. The rock fractures and releases the petroleum. The horizontal shafts allow shallow lenses to be exploited and also allow access to hard-to-reach deposits. This in turn has increased domestic production of oil and brought down gasoline prices.

Unfortunately, fracking raises several environmental concerns. Because the process involves forcing jets of water down long shafts, it uses enormous amounts of water, from 1.5 to 16 million gallons (5.7 to 60.6 million L) per well.[3] The chemicals used in fracking may cause cancer, and critics worry these chemicals could find their way into the water supply. Finally, earthquakes are a problem in areas where fracking occurs. In September 2016, a magnitude 5.6 earthquake struck Oklahoma, tying the record for strongest Oklahoma earthquake. Scientists say the quake was not caused directly by fracking but by the storage of wastewater from fracked and non-fracked wells in the earth.

ECONOMIC BLISS

Many people believe fracking is worth the risks. For one thing, it has created a boom in production of Bakken crude. In the past decade, North Dakota has become the second-biggest oil producer in the United States, behind only Texas. Between 2006 and 2014, oil output in the Bakken region increased twelvefold.[4] This boom in production flooded the market with cheap oil. This oversupply meant there was more oil to sell, so the price dropped.

This has made it harder for smaller oil companies to make big profits, but the pipeline is seen as a solution to this problem. Because North Dakota is so far from the major oil markets, producing the oil is only the first step. To get the oil to where it can be refined and turned into usable products, it must be transported by train, truck, or pipeline, which is why ETP is building DAPL.

DONE AND GONE

One reason supporters say the pipeline is good for North Dakota is job creation. The pipeline required up to 12,000 people to construct it, but that was only in the building phase when workers were needed to dig trenches and install and weld pipe. The jobs disappear when the construction work is complete. The pipeline owners estimate DAPL will provide 40 ongoing full-time jobs.[5]

Even in construction, the pipeline has positively impacted the economy. ETP executive Joey Mahmoud told reporters that more than $1 billion in pipe and other equipment was contracted from various US companies in early 2016. "Everything except for a couple of pumps and a little bit of pipe was made here in the United States," Mahmoud said. He continued:

> From a manufacturing standpoint, the project has been a huge boost, so it's not just from a labor standpoint. All the materials that possibly could have been sourced were right here, so an overall $3–4 billion job like this has a total impact of about $20 billion on the economy. This is a huge windfall for our country, and we're pretty fortunate to be able to develop this project that will need about 12,000 construction workers by the time it's finished in early 2017.[6]

The economic benefits will continue as the pipeline moves into operation. It is estimated that the pipeline will transport between 450,000 and 570,000 barrels per day.

PRICE PER BARREL

When ETP negotiated the contract to build DAPL, the company agreed to have the pipeline finished and operational by December 2016. Oil refiners, for their part, agreed to buy the crude oil from the pipeline for a set price—the price of oil in 2014. In 2014, that price was $70 to $80 per barrel. Because ETP failed to complete the pipeline by December, the company had to renegotiate the contract for the price of oil in 2017, which is $40 to $50 per barrel.[7]

Oil trucks and new housing developments are evidence of the oil boom in North Dakota.

A barrel is 42 gallons (159 L), so this translates to 18.9 to 23.9 million gallons (71.5 to 90.5 million L) per day. This is half of the average daily Bakken production.[8] Taxation of this oil will generate an estimated $50 million in property taxes and $74 million in sales taxes per year.[9] Because it costs less to transport oil by pipeline, oil companies will earn more than if the oil were trucked or transported by train. Ron Ness, president of the North Dakota Petroleum

OIL RIG SAFETY

On average, a worker dies every six weeks in the Bakken oil fields.[11] On September 14, 2011, 21-year-old Brendan Wegner burned to death on his first day working on an oil rig. He died when a blowout shot oil 50 feet (15.2 m) into the air and the rig caught on fire. As derrick man, Wegner's job was to connect and disconnect piping high off the ground, but the company that built the rig failed to install an emergency egress line, similar to a zip line that enables workers to escape in an emergency. Although the US Occupational Safety and Health Administration (OSHA) has rules about workplace safety, oil companies avoid compliance by hiring multiple contractors. One company builds the oil rig, another hires the workers, and still another supervises daily operation. This makes it difficult for OSHA to discover who is responsible for a specific safety violation and hold that company responsible. When asked about the dangers of working Bakken, Kari Cutting, vice president of the North Dakota Petroleum Council, said, "I do not have any facts that would lead me to the conclusion that there are major concerns. . . . I think North Dakota is very much in line with other states as far as putting safety as priority one."[12]

Council, stated that this savings in transportation costs could be as much as three dollars per barrel.

SAFETY FIRST

Not only is the pipeline the less expensive means of transportation, ETP also says it is the safest way to transport crude oil, safer and with less environmental harm than trains or trucks. It contends, "Monitored 24/7/365, federal statistics show that underground pipelines transport crude oil more safely than rail (3.4–4.5x safer) or trucks (34x safer)."[10]

But no pipeline is immune to accidents. A memo written by Hilary Tompkins, who was a top lawyer for the Department of the Interior under the Obama administration, points out that the Pipeline and Hazardous Materials Safety Administration tracks serious

pipeline incidents, and "their data indicates that since 1996, there has been an average of over 283 such incidents per year, with total annual incidents trending upward since 2013."[13] In July 2010, for example, a leak in the Enbridge pipeline in Calhoun County, Michigan, led to a discharge of 800,000 gallons (3,000,000 L) of crude oil into the Kalamazoo River, requiring emergency evacuations of local residents, injuring birds and other wildlife, contaminating more than 30 miles of river, and requiring cleanup on the order of $1.2 billion.[14] The risk of this kind of disaster is one of the factors that led the water protectors from Standing Rock to object to DAPL.

CHAPTER THREE

RESERVATION
LANDS

T he Lakota and Dakota live at Standing Rock and several other reservations, as well as in cities and towns throughout the country. They are two of the groups that make up the Sioux, a confederacy of tribes with similar customs and languages. The name *Sioux* originated with the Ojibwe word *Nadowe-is-iw-ug*, meaning "little adders," which are a type of snake. The Ojibwe were enemies of the Sioux but allies of the French, and a French mispronunciation, *Nadewisou*, of this derogatory Ojibwe name for their enemies is the source of the name still in use today.

At one time, Sioux peoples occupied the land from Wyoming in the west to Wisconsin in the east, north into Canada and as far south as Kansas. French fur

Swiss artist Karl Bodmer painted his impression of Sioux tepees in 1833.

traders arrived in the Great Lakes region in the 1660s and allied with the Ojibwe, offering trade goods, including guns, in exchange for furs. But as the Ojibwe exhausted the fur-bearing animals in their own territory, they ventured west in search of animals to trap, and they soon pushed their way into Sioux lands. As the groups fought over the land, the Sioux peoples lost one skirmish after another. Eventually, the Lakota moved westward away from this fighting. By the mid-1700s, they had acquired horses and settled in North Dakota around the sacred Black Hills.

THE SACRED BLACK HILLS

The Black Hills are sacred to the Lakota. The Lakota name for this area is Paha Sapa, which in their language means "the heart of everything that is." These hills are where the Lakota came into being. "All of our origin stories go back to this place. We have a spiritual connection to the Black Hills that can't be sold. I don't think I could face the Creator with an open heart if I ever took money for it," said Rick Two-Dogs, an Oglala Lakota elder.[1]

HORSEMEN OF THE PLAINS

From 1775 to 1868, the Lakota lived on roughly 100 million acres (40 million ha) of the Great Plains. They rode horses as they hunted the enormous herds of bison, sewing together bison hides to create tepee covers and clothing and making tools from the animals' bones. The people had no towns but followed the buffalo, so they owned no more than they could pull loaded on travois behind their horses.

By 1840, land-hungry Americans were moving west in wagon trains. As group after group traveled through the territory of the Lakota, the migrating settlers grazed their livestock where the bison normally fed, thus pushing these essential animals out of Lakota territory. The Lakota tried threatening and then attacking the wagon trains to get whites to stay out of their territory, but nothing worked to preserve the bison or stem the tide of outsiders.

FORT LARAMIE TREATIES

The government solution to the Lakota threat against invading wagon trains was to confine the group onto reservations. To implement this plan, the US government offered to negotiate, and the Lakota and other Native Americans gathered at Fort Laramie, Wyoming, to sign the treaty. In the 1851 treaty, the Lakota agreed to stop harassing the wagon trains and to stay on the lands reserved for them, 60 million acres (24 million ha) that included the Black Hills. The US government would help feed the Lakota by giving them an annual allotment of cattle, farm equipment, seeds, and grain for ten years, planning to turn the people from hunters into farmers.

However, it proved impossible to prevent whites from entering Lakota lands. Gold had been discovered in Colorado in 1859, and there were rumors by 1861 that Montana also contained gold. People seeking gold headed into the treaty lands guaranteed to the various groups of Sioux. The Sioux fought back in what came to be called

WAGONS WEST

In 1841, 70 American settlers made up the first wagon train that started down the Oregon Trail, a 2,140-mile (3,440 km) route that left Missouri and then split to either California or Oregon. In 1842, a second wagon train left with 100 people. On May 22, 1843, the first large train, consisting of 1,000 people, 100 wagons, and the 5,000 horses and oxen used to pull the wagons, left Elm Grove, Missouri.[2] Before the transcontinental railroad was completed in 1869, more than 500,000 people and their livestock completed the trip by wagon, using the resources needed by the bison and the Lakota.[3]

Red Cloud's War, named for the Oglala chief who led the Sioux fighters.

Congress wanted to build a road for gold prospectors in the Montana gold district, but before this could happen the fighting needed to stop. Peace talks convened, and the resulting Treaty of 1868 granted the Lakota the Great Sioux Reservation, which included half of South Dakota and parts of Nebraska and Wyoming. The treaty stated, "No white person, or persons, shall be permitted to settle upon or occupy any portion of the territory, or without consent of the Indians . . . to pass through the same."[4] The Lakota hoped this time their rights would be respected.

Interaction between the Lakota and whites was to take place through the Indian Agency. This was a government trade outpost that oversaw trade between whites and the various tribes including, in this area, the Lakota. The agent in charge was a government employee who verified that federal trade policy was put into effect and also settled disputes among the tribes and the local white population. Later the agent also encouraged Native Americans to give up hunting and take up farming, settling down on the reservations and living like whites. What is now the

Standing Rock Agency was first named the Grand River Agency in 1868 and was located on the banks of the Grand River in South Dakota. In 1874, it was relocated to the US Army outpost of Fort Yates, North Dakota, and renamed Standing Rock. Today located in the Standing Rock Reservation, people still come to the agency for health care and other services.

BISON HUNTING

No one is certain how many bison once roamed the plains of the United States. Estimates range from 30 to 60 million. By the late 1800s, only a few hundred wild bison remained because they had been intentionally slaughtered to destroy the Native Americans. As explained in 1873 by Columbus Delano, Secretary of the Interior, "I would not seriously regret the total disappearance of the buffalo from our western plains, in its effect upon the Indians."[5] Railroads offered hunting specials—ride the rails and shoot bison, stopping only long enough to harvest the hide and tongue. The rest was left to rot in the sun. As one army colonel said, "Kill every buffalo you can! Every buffalo dead is an Indian gone."[6]

GOLD IN THE BLACK HILLS

In 1874, Lieutenant Colonel George Armstrong Custer violated the Treaty of 1868 by leading an illegal military expedition into the Black Hills to investigate a location for a new fort. His force also scouted for and found gold. Soon, gold seekers were coming to prospect for gold and cut down woodlands to build towns and camps. When the Sioux threatened to attack, these illegal settlers demanded the US government remove the Sioux from the area.

The government first tried to buy the Black Hills, but the Lakota were not interested in selling this sacred land. Hunkpapa Sioux chief Sitting Bull said, "We want no white men here. The Black Hills belong to me. If the whites try to take them, I will fight."[7] Gold prospectors continued to enter the Sioux lands, and the US Army was determined to protect the interlopers, but the Sioux fought back.

As the weather warmed in 1876, Sioux bands gathered in larger and larger numbers. An enormous tepee village of up to 10,000 people grew near the Little Big Horn River. Custer tracked them to this location and attacked. Chief Sitting Bull and Chief Gall led the Hunkpapa Sioux while Chief Crazy Horse led the Oglala, yelling as he rode into battle, "Come on,

CRAZY HORSE

Crazy Horse, known in his own language as Tashunka Witko, was a leader among the Lakota Sioux. He led his fighters into battle to keep his people from being forced to live on reservations. He sometimes acted as a decoy to lead US Army units into ambushes. At Little Bighorn in 1876, his troops fought in the battle that defeated Custer. He and his people finally surrendered on May 6, 1877. While they were awaiting assignment to a reservation, rumors spread that he was planning to lead men into battle again. This led to his arrest on September 5, during which he was stabbed to death.

Lakotas! It's a good day to die."[8] By the conclusion of the battle, which lasted from June 25 to June 26, 1876, Custer and all of his men lay dead.

Although the Lakota and other Sioux won this particular battle, Custer's defeat led many Americans to demand the genocide of the Sioux. Throughout the fall and winter of that year, US army units pursued bands of Sioux through the hills as the government threatened to remove them to Indian Territory in modern Oklahoma. By mid-1877, many chiefs, including Red Cloud, had surrendered and signed a treaty that gave the Black Hills to the government.

THE GREAT SIOUX RESERVATION DISMANTLED

In the late 1880s, as the Dakota Territories were on the verge of becoming the states of North and South Dakota, many whites who lived in the area called for the Great Sioux Reservation to be reduced or dismantled. This acreage had been promised to the Lakota and other Sioux people now living there. But whites saw 43,000 square miles (110,000 sq km) of land they believed should be settled by farmers and developed in ways that would benefit the economy.[9]

In 1888, representatives of the federal government visited groups of Sioux and attempted to get them to agree with the Sioux Bill, a law that called for the breakup of the Great Sioux Reservation into smaller reservations, the forfeiture of nine million acres (3.6 million ha) of land, the creation of land allotments for Sioux families, and the sale of nonallotted land to outsiders.[10] The representatives needed adult men over the age of 18 to sign the document. According to the Fort Laramie Treaty of 1868, they needed signatures from three-quarters of all adult Sioux males to approve the bill, and they started seeking signatures in Standing Rock. The majority refused to sign because they wanted to keep what was left of their lands.

"YOU HAVE DRIVEN AWAY OUR GAME AND OUR MEANS OF LIVELIHOOD OUT OF THE COUNTRY, UNTIL NOW WE HAVE NOTHING LEFT THAT IS VALUABLE EXCEPT THE HILLS THAT YOU ASK US TO GIVE UP. . . . THE EARTH IS FULL OF MINERALS OF ALL KINDS, AND ON THE EARTH THE GROUND IS COVERED WITH FORESTS OF HEAVY PINE, AND WHEN WE GIVE THESE UP TO THE GREAT FATHER WE KNOW THAT WE GIVE UP THE LAST THING THAT IS VALUABLE EITHER TO US OR THE WHITE PEOPLE."[11]

—CHIEF WANIGI SKA (WHITE GHOST) OF THE LOWER YAKTONAI SIOUX ON THE SALE OF THE BLACK HILLS

In 1889, government representatives again undertook the task of gathering signatures, but this time they came with threats. If the men did not sign the bill, the government would take all of their land, not just part of it. The representatives would not take no for an answer, and eventually people started signing. Standing Rock was the last agency the representatives visited. One-half of the adult men signed the bill, and, combined with the signatures already collected, this was enough to dismantle the Great Sioux Reservation. Six separate reservations were created, including Standing Rock. Events showed that previous treaties meant little as long as the Lakota had something the United States valued enough to take away.

EDUCATED WHITE

War and forced settlement weren't the only methods the government used to break Native Americans. They also used education at off-reservation boarding schools. In 1879, the first boarding school, the Carlisle Indian Industrial School, was founded in Carlisle, Pennsylvania. School founder Richard Pratt had a motto—kill the Indian, save

Lakota leaders pose at Standing Rock Reservation in the 1880s.

the man. The goal of Carlisle and schools like it was to remove every aspect of native culture.

Native American children from all over the country were shipped to schools like Carlisle. Stripped of traditional clothing, their hair was cut, and they were given white names. English was the only language they were allowed to speak, and anyone who spoke a native language, even if they knew no other, was beaten.

Children were still being removed from their homes well into the 1900s. "The nuns and the priests and the Indian agent; they came and they took me and my brother away in 1934. My mom, she tried to resist, but if you do that, you're going to go to jail," said Albert Taylor, a member of the Sioux Valley Dakota Nation.[12] It wasn't until 1978 with the passage of the Indian Child Welfare Act that Native American parents could refuse to let their children be taken to these schools.

These harsh tactics helped give rise to the native rights movement and the founding of the American Indian Movement (AIM) in 1968. Originally, the group worked to help Native Americans who had been moved from the reservations to poor urban neighborhoods. The group

Students at the Carlisle school, 1890s

revitalized traditional cultures, helped people support themselves without government aid, and protected the legal rights of Native Americans. It demanded the return of traditional lands including the Black Hills and called for the Lakota and Dakota to have a say in how their lives and their land was managed.

Today, the Standing Rock Sioux Tribe governs itself as a sovereign nation, standing on equal footing with the state and federal governments. Its constitution was approved in 1959. Tribal government manages the tribe's property, makes laws, and hears court cases. The tribe also holds jurisdiction over all waterways on the reservation lands.

CHAPTER FOUR

INDIGENOUS
RIGHTS

Because Standing Rock is a federal Indian reservation, the land has been set aside, or reserved, for the use of the tribe under a treaty between the tribe and the US government. Some reservation lands, such as the lands originally granted to the Cherokee, Choctaw, and Chickasaw Nations in the Oklahoma Territory, were given to a tribe for resettlement when the tribe was forced from its original homelands. Other reservations, such as Standing Rock, are part of a tribe's traditional lands even if the area represents only a small fraction of the land the tribe once utilized.

The tribe does not own reservation land; the federal government holds the land in trust for the tribe. The

Standing Rock Sioux chair Dave Archambault II was a leader of the protests and legal action against DAPL.

government is required by law to protect treaty rights, the land itself, and any land-based assets and resources. The Supreme Court has indicated that this is not only a legal obligation but also a moral duty. Because of the obligations the US government has to protect the treaty rights of the Standing Rock nation, the tribe called upon the government to preserve the land around Lake Oahe. The US government isn't dealing with just another group of citizens. Legally, any tribe recognized by the government has sovereignty. This means they are independent nations with the right to govern themselves and meet the needs of their people. The US government was dealing government-to-government regarding the land around Lake Oahe.

Critics of the tribe point out that the land in question is not within the boundaries of the reservation. While the

INDIAN LANDS IN TRUST

The federal government holds approximately 56.2 million acres (22.7 million ha) of land in trust for a variety of tribes. This acreage is split into roughly 300 reservations ranging in size from the 16-million-acre (6.5 million ha) Navajo Nation in Arizona, New Mexico, and Utah, to the 1.32-acre (0.53 ha) Likely Rancheria in California, which serves as a cemetery for the Pit River Tribe.[1] Although all of the land is technically reservation land, not all of them are called reservations. There are also pueblos, villages, missions, and rancherías.

pipeline does run outside of the reservation as it is defined today, the land in question was supposed to be part of the reservation as defined by the Fort Laramie Treaty of 1851. Although representatives of both the tribe and the federal government signed this treaty, some of the land promised to the tribe, including the land where the pipeline runs, was never ceded over for the tribe's use. Whether or not the land is part of the current reservation, it is part of the tribe's traditional land base. As such, people who support indigenous rights feel the tribe should have a stronger say in what happens on that land.

FISHING AND HUNTING RIGHTS

Although Lake Oahe is not on the Standing Rock Reservation, this body of water does border the reservation, and the tribe retains both fishing and hunting rights to the lake. Both the UN and human rights organization Amnesty International work to help guarantee fishing and hunting grounds for indigenous people such as those living on Standing Rock. These organizations do this with the understanding that traditional sources of food are often essential to people who are trying to feed their families. Without access to these areas, or should these areas be damaged, food could become insecure, thus contributing to malnutrition and health problems.

PRIVATIZATION

Although reservations encompass somewhat more than 56 million acres (23 million ha) in the United States, this accounts for just two percent of US land. However, this small fraction of land may contain 20 percent of the remaining oil, gas, and coal reserves in the country.[2] Not all tribes are opposed to using their lands to extract and transport energy resources. The Crow Indian Reservation in Montana mines the coal reserves that lie beneath the surface of its land. These mines generate income for the tribe and provide jobs for reservation residents. In contrast, the Cheyenne tribe, whose reservation shares a border with the Crow reservation and also sits on top of coal reserves, is against mining on its land.

Although the tribes do not own their reservations outright, they can drill and mine and otherwise take advantage of the minerals on that land if they choose to do so. Because the reservations are federal property, the laws controlling how to access these reserves are more complicated than laws concerning mining on private property. President Donald Trump and his advisers want to get rid of regulations they feel hamper energy production. One way they seek to do this would be to privatize the reservations. This would make the rules about drilling the land less complicated, but it could also mean that reservation lands could be sold to non-Natives.

Many Native Americans object to this plan. "Our spiritual leaders are opposed to the privatization of our lands, which means the commoditization of the nature, water, air we hold sacred," said Tom Goldtooth, a member of both the Navajo and the Dakota tribes who runs the Indigenous Environmental Network. "Privatization has been the goal since colonization—to strip Native Nations of their sovereignty."[3] Those opposed to privatization feel that such actions represent institutional racism.

WHAT IS PRIVATIZATION?

Privatization takes place any time ownership or management of something is transferred from the government to an individual or group. Transferring reservation lands from government to individual ownership, whether or not the individuals are members of the tribe, is one way to privatize land. The 1887 Dawes Act caused a large amount of reservation lands to be privatized. The act offered land parcels for individual Native families and people that they would own outright after 25 years and granted the people who accepted the land US citizenship. The effect was to take power and unity away from the tribes and encourage the new citizens to assimilate into white culture, causing a rift between those who took the offer and those who did not. The new landowners could also sell their land, leading to a patchwork of non-Native-owned lands within reservation borders.

Indigenous people from far and near joined the camp at Standing Rock, including these members of the Quinault Nation from Washington State wearing wolf masks during a protest demonstration.

INSTITUTIONAL RACISM

Racism is any act of prejudice or discrimination in which people identified as one race are treated differently than people identified as another race. It can include stereotyping people or ignoring someone's concerns. When racism is built into the institutions that make up a government or society, it is called institutional or structural racism.

The original path of DAPL took it near the Bismarck water supply, but when residents objected that this was a danger to their drinking water, ETP moved the pipeline to the present location near Standing Rock. The residents of Bismarck are 92 percent white.[4]

When the Native American residents of Standing Rock objected to the danger to their water supply as well as to Lake Oahe and the Missouri River, ETP executives stated the pipeline would be perfectly safe. Protecting the group in power, in this case white Americans, by endangering a group that has less power, the Standing Rock Sioux, may be an example of institutional racism.

"NO MATTER WHERE YOU ARE IN THE WORLD, INDIGENOUS PEOPLE TALK ABOUT . . . FOSSIL FUEL PROJECTS COMING IN AND DESTROYING THEIR HOMELANDS, THREATENING THEIR DRINKING WATER, THREATENING THEIR FUTURE. . . . STANDING ROCK HAS BECOME FOR INDIGENOUS PEOPLE THIS MOMENT WHERE THEY ARE ALL STANDING TOGETHER BECAUSE THEY ALL KNOW WHAT HAPPENS WHEN SOMETHING LIKE THIS IS ALLOWED TO HAPPEN TO THEM."[5]

—TARA HOUSKA, DIRECTOR, HONOR THE EARTH

It is because of this type of racism that the United Nations (UN) adopted the Declaration on the Rights of Indigenous Peoples in 2007. The UN is an international organization that helps countries negotiate with each other and facilitates international action. The declaration is an 11-page document that defines the rights of indigenous people worldwide, including the right to be equal to other people while simultaneously living differently than they do. These differences in how people live, says the declaration, contribute to the richness of civilization. In addition, the UN considers any law that puts one group ahead of another to be racist, unjust, and immoral. The declaration also asserts that indigenous people have the right to organize politically to rid themselves of the many racist policies that work against them. Perhaps most importantly for DAPL, this document states that indigenous people should have control over developments that affect them and their lands.

INDIGENOUS?

The World Health Organization (WHO) defines an indigenous community as any community that lives within or identifies with a specific geographic habitat, such as the Lakota living in and identifying with the Black Hills. The definition also specifies a distinct culture or set of beliefs that encompasses language, religion, and material possessions such as clothing, homes, and tools. An indigenous people is also one that is descended from people who lived in the geographic area before modern governments ruled there, such as the Lakota, who lived in the Black Hills before the United States or the state of North Dakota effectively governed the area.

An anti-DAPL protest in New York City in the spring of 2017 emphasized the need to recognize indigenous sovereignty.

The UN worked for 20 years to pass this document because the issues it touches are vital on a global scale. These problems include development and how it can be carried out in a way that is not racist to a segment of the society that lacks power, the decentralization of power so that it is not held by one ethnic group but by many, and the need for multicultural democracy. The idea is that only when everyone in a diverse society, such as the United States, has access to and benefits from the government will that government be able to work toward the good of all its people—whether it is a matter of access to energy, jobs, or clean water.

CHAPTER FIVE

WATER
SAFETY

I n the 1960s, citizens across the United States pushed
the government to create agencies to help regulate
pollution and the environment. In 1962, biologist
Rachel Carson published *Silent Spring*. The book showed
the general public the links biologists had made
between the pesticide DDT and the failure of eagles,
falcons, and other birds to hatch chicks. This was the
first time many people realized the chemicals sprayed
on farms could affect wildlife miles away.

People were talking about ecology, and politicians
responded. First came the 1970 passage of the National
Environmental Policy Act, which created the Council
on Environmental Quality. For the first time, studies
into the environmental impact would be required

As part of Americans' growing environmental consciousness, the first
Earth Day was celebrated on April 22, 1970.

whenever a federal agency planned a project that could alter the environment wherever the project took place. President Richard Nixon established the US Environmental Protection Agency (EPA) on December 2, 1970. This government agency was tasked with creating policies and enforcing many environmental laws created by Congress, including the Clean Water Act of 1972.

Many scientists credit *Silent Spring* for launching the modern environmental movement and also making it a partisan issue. People openly took sides in support of their cause, the environment in opposition to big business. DAPL made it clear this deep divide is still present.

COMPANIES IN COURT

After *Silent Spring* was published and new environmental

DDT

DDT was developed in the 1940s as the first man-made insecticide. It was used in the military and also among civilians to control the mosquitoes that carried malaria and typhus, two deadly viruses. It was also used to control insects that ate crops, gardens, and plants in people's yards, and to eliminate insects that spread livestock-related diseases. As it killed off the insects that were most susceptible to it, the surviving insects reproduced, and subsequent generations were more and more resistant. DDT also had devastating effects on birds, almost leading to the extinction of species including the bald eagle and peregrine falcon. In response to these concerns, the use of DDT for agricultural purposes was banned in the United States in 1972.

policies came into play, chemical companies fought back, publishing a parody making fun of the beginning of Carson's book. They also started negotiations with the US government. The companies that produced DDT were willing to quit selling DDT in the United States if they could still sell it in other countries.

Fossil fuel companies are just as savvy when it comes to finding ways around the laws that regulate their industry. For example, as fracking has grown more common, environmentalists and concerned citizens have demanded to know what chemical compounds are combined with the water used to release oil from the shale formations. Under a 1986 law, the Emergency Planning and Community Right to Know Act, industries must release information to neighboring communities about the chemicals they are using that might affect the health and well-being of these communities. Emergency responders in particular need to know which chemicals they might be exposed to when responding to chemical incidents. One nurse, Cathy Behr, almost died after she helped a worker whose clothes were soaked in fracking fluid. But fracking companies say that revealing the chemicals they use would be revealing trade secrets to their competitors and harmful to their businesses if they were forced to comply.

DAPL AND THE ENVIRONMENT

ETP stands by its assessment that DAPL will be safe for the environment, as well as its human neighbors. In multiple statements, ETP explained that it listened to Standing Rock residents' concerns regarding the safety of their drinking water, but that these concerns are unfounded for several reasons. Other energy-transportation infrastructure exists in the area of the lake, including high-voltage electrical lines strung overhead on towers, and, perhaps most importantly from the perspective of a pipeline company, several pipelines already pass beneath the lake. DAPL was to be laid below these existing pipelines, at a depth of up to 115 feet (35 m). At 20 miles (32 km) away, the pipeline is far enough from the intake that draws the tribe's water that the company asserts DAPL will pose no water supply problems even if there is a spill.

The other reason ETP gives for knowing that the tribe's water will remain safe is that the tribe now uses a new water intake. In early 2017, the tribe started using a

Lake Oahe, formed by a dam on the Missouri River, is one of the largest artificial reservoirs in the United States.

water treatment plant that draws water 70 miles (110 km) away from the pipeline. Because it is estimated that the Missouri River flows at a speed from about five to eight miles per hour (8 to 13 kmh), in the event of a spill it would take the oil nine to fourteen hours to reach the new intake. This should give the tribe sufficient time to close a valve and prevent contaminated water from entering its plant. "The new intake really does effectively reduce the concerns that this oil pipeline could impact the tribe's water supply," said Julie Fedorchak, head of North Dakota's Public Service Commission, which approved the pipeline.[1]

While perhaps reducing the threat of a spill to the tribe's water supply, the new water

LEAK DETECTION

Perhaps the easiest way to test a lengthy pipeline for leaks involves installing monitoring equipment in a maintenance tool known as a pipeline pig. As the canister-shaped pig travels through the pipeline, its instruments gather information. In the magnetic flux method, a strong permanent magnet magnetizes the pipeline. Changes in the pipeline's magnetic field, or flux, captured by sensors in the pig show where corrosion has damaged the pipeline. In the ultrasonic method, equipment in the pig transmits ultrasonic pulses and receives reflected signals, which allow wall thickness to be calculated. To monitor the pipeline externally, equipment for acoustic monitoring can also be set up along the pipeline. When liquids flow through a crack or hole in a pipeline, they make a sound these sensors can capture. However, a large number of sensors are needed to monitor long pipes, and minor leaks go undetected because setting the sensors to catch small leaks yields too many false alarms.

intake does not eliminate this threat. For example, in the Enbridge spill in 2010 in Michigan, crude oil leaked from the pipeline for more than 17 hours before operators shut it down. A leak of 17 hours from DAPL could be sufficient to contaminate the sole source of drinking water for the Standing Rock tribe. Even if the tribe closes its intake valve in time to avoid contamination at the plant, it would need to find a different source of water.

INSUFFICIENT EVIDENCE

Despite the many reasons that ETP gave to show the pipeline poses no danger to water, critics disagree because a full environmental impact statement was never completed. Whenever a building project such as a road, bridge, or pipeline crosses federal land and affects a federal waterway, the

WHEN ACCIDENTS HAPPEN

When the Husky Energy oil pipeline ruptured on July 21, 2016, 66,000 gallons (250,000 L) of heavy oil poured into the North Saskatchewan River in the province of Saskatchewan, Canada.[2] The town of North Battleford shut off its intake valve and started using groundwater to meet the needs of its citizens. The larger city of Prince Albert shut down its treatment plant and had enough water stored to last its citizens for two days if they limited how much they used. By then, the city had laid a temporary pipeline to draw water from the South Saskatchewan River. Residents were fortunate their leaders found ways to work around the contaminated water.

USACE typically has to complete a study of all cultural and environmental impacts. This means the agency needs to note what may be damaged or destroyed in the completion of a proposed project—whether it is cultural, such as a historic building or a burial ground, or environmental, such as a fragile ecosystem or body of water. The USACE didn't complete a full study for DAPL, as it announced it would do near the end of the Obama administration.

Even where the pipeline crosses the Missouri River at Lake Oahe, a full assessment was not done. To get the permission required to build this portion of the pipeline, ETP sought approval under Nationwide Permit No. 12, which usually does not require a full environmental impact study. Instead, the USACE focused its surveys only on the small area near the pipeline crossing, not the watershed as a whole, even though the greater region might be damaged if there were a spill.

ABATEMENT ERRORS

Even a Nationwide Permit No. 12 requires some environmental impact information, and in the case of a

MORE TO THE
STORY

NATIONWIDE PERMIT 12

The USACE Nationwide Permit No. 12 arises under the legal authority of the federal Clean Water Act. The Clean Water Act generally prohibits the pollution of water in lakes, rivers, streams, and the ocean without a permit from either the US Environmental Protection Agency or the USACE, or from states or tribes who received special authorization to issue permits.

It can take a long time, sometimes years, to get a permit to discharge pollution under the Clean Water Act, as a number of studies and opportunities for public comments may be required before the permit can be issued. One way that agencies try to make this process faster is by using standardized permits for certain kinds of projects. In essence, if you agree to certain conditions specified in the standard permit, you simply get the permit.

Nationwide Permit No. 12 is one of these standardized permits used by the USACE. It is used for small utility line projects that impact 0.5 acres (0.2 ha) or less of water for the entire project. This permit is frequently used for projects that have to do with energy development. Supporters of this permit process state that rules regarding permit use comply with the Clean Water Act, but opponents disagree. "We think the way that it's currently written is contrary to the Clean Water Act," said Jim Murphy, National Wildlife Federation lead counsel.[3] Because the nationwide permit process looks at each water crossing individually, there is no study of a project's overall impact.

pipeline it is supposed to include plans for abatement, or cleaning up a spill, should one occur. However, critics including Jennifer Veilleux, an international water security and transboundary river post-doctoral researcher at Florida International University in Miami, Florida, believe the information in the report is insufficient compared to what would have to be done if a spill did occur.

Because of oil's tendency to float, the report included abatement information for cleaning up floating oil. The problem is that the pipeline, as built by ETP, is not at the surface of the lake but buried deep below the lake floor. Because it is buried underground, spilled oil would first pass through soil, where it would bind to the sediment. The environmental impact report completed by ETP and the

CORROSIVE CRUDE

The journal *Materials Performance* interviewed a panel of scientists who work in the oil and gas industry about the tendency for oil pipelines to corrode. The scientists agreed that it isn't the crude itself that is corrosive at the temperatures found within a pipeline. Crude oil becomes corrosive only when it is heated, as happens in a refinery. Rather, the corrosion comes from solid particles and water. The particles are suspended in the oil when it enters the pipeline but settle as the oil moves down the pipe. If these particles contain water, this water is then pressed against the surface of the pipeline, where it can lead to surface pitting. Heavy crude can safely travel more slowly than light crude without these particles settling to the bottom of the pipe.

USACE includes no study of the impact this oil would have on the soil or the organisms living in it, and no plans have been made concerning cleaning the sediment of spilled oil. This part of the environment has been completely left out of the study and the report, and this worries Veilleux because of the tendency pipelines have to corrode. Not everyone shares her concerns, however, and many believe the risks are worth the energy the pipeline will provide.

FROM THE HEADLINES

IT ISN'T JUST OIL THREATENING DRINKING WATER

Oil isn't the only dangerous material related to drilling that can leak and cause damage. To frack one oil well requires from 1.5 to 16 million gallons (5.7 to 60.6 million L) of water.[4] This water is combined with a variety of other substances, including petroleum products such as diesel fuel and kerosene. The brine, or wastewater, is stored in on-site tanks until it can be transported by truck or pipeline to various storage options, including permanent deep wells.

On January 6, 2015, 3 million gallons (11 million L) of brine leaked near the town of Williston, North Dakota.[5] The spill contaminated two creeks, and, although no drinking water was immediately affected, farmers were warned to keep their livestock away from the affected creeks. Because the spill took place in winter, the water and soil were frozen, and it was impossible to judge the extent of the contamination and damage. Typical mitigation for a spill includes draining smaller creeks and removing any soil that tests positive for contaminants. Larger creeks are

Crews build a sandbag dam to contain the spill
on the Fort Berthold Reservation in 2014.

not drained because naturally occurring water is expected to dilute the level of salt in the water to acceptable levels.

In July 2014, a similar leak took place when a pipeline carrying Bakken brine ruptured. The chemical-laden water poured down Bear Den Ravine on the Fort Berthold Reservation in western North Dakota. The ravine forms a Missouri River tributary and is less than 0.5 miles (0.8 km) from the Mandaree water-intake system. Vance Gillette, a former chief judge of the Mandan, Hidatsa, and Arikara Nation, was on the scene from the early moments of the spill. "When I reached the site where the spill occurred, the water near the bay was a rusted color and the shoreline vegetation was dying," he said. "From what I saw at the spill site, it is highly unlikely the results of the water tests will show no contamination."[6]

CHAPTER SIX

THE PRICE
OF OIL

I n 2016, petroleum made up 37 percent of the energy consumed annually in the United States.[1] One thing President Trump promised voters during his campaign was that he would help the United States break away from dependence on oil from the Organization of Petroleum Exporting Countries (OPEC). OPEC is an international organization that works to coordinate the petroleum policies of member countries, including Venezuela, Iran, Iraq, and Saudi Arabia. As stated in the energy plan posted on the White House website, "The Trump Administration is committed to energy policies that lower costs for hardworking Americans and

Oil derricks that pump up oil from underground dot the landscape in North Dakota.

maximize the use of American resources, freeing us from dependence on foreign oil."[2]

In Trump's plan, this means replacing imports of foreign oil with domestically produced oil, such as Bakken crude. The reasoning is that fracking gives the United States access to domestic sources of oil that would otherwise remain inaccessible. Developing domestic oil keeps prices low because it costs less than overseas oil. Domestic oil also reduces dependence on foreign oil, which, in turn, makes the United States more energy independent, heightening security.

In addition to giving the United States access to oil supplies that cannot be cut off at the whim of a foreign power, reliance on domestic oil would also contribute to economic stability. The money used to purchase imported oil makes up nearly two-thirds of the United States' annual trade deficit.[3] In January 2017, largely due to rising international oil prices, that trade deficit reached $48.5 billion.[4] If the nation could stop importing oil, this money could be put to work within the United States instead of going to benefit a foreign country.

MORE TO THE
STORY

CLIMATE CHANGE
THREATENS SECURITY

Even as the United States finds new ways to access its oil, climate change is threatening the nation's energy security. Part of the problem comes with the global warming that is a part of climate change. When temperatures are higher, people use more electricity and therefore more energy, running their air conditioners and fans so that they can stay cool. Rising temperatures and changing weather patterns are also linked to a pattern of more intense storms, including hurricanes, which interrupt oil and gas operations when workers have to shut things down to seek shelter. Furthermore, changing rainfall and snowfall has changed water availability in areas that use hydropower even as storms and wildfires disrupt the nation's electric grid.

It isn't just energy that is at risk. Rising sea levels threaten 128 US military bases, some of which have already flooded.[5] In addition, rising water levels and extreme weather are causing hardship in poverty stricken parts of the world. This allows extreme political groups to more easily gain power, threatening global security. Seventeen retired military officers wrote a letter asking Secretary of State Rex Tillerson and Defense Secretary James Mattis to continue US efforts to combat climate change. They believe US national security depends on recognizing the dangers posed by the warming planet.

Trump isn't the only president to see the benefits of developing sources of US oil. In his 2013 State of the Union address, President Barack Obama spoke about increased domestic production: "After years of talking about it, we are finally poised to control our own energy future."[6]

BAKKEN BASICS

The United States Geological Survey (USGS) has estimated the Bakken formation contains anywhere from 4.4 to 11.4 billion barrels of oil that can be recovered based on the technology now in use. How long this oil will last depends on how quickly it is extracted. Approximately 450 million barrels of Bakken oil were removed between 2008 and 2013.[7]

The problem isn't entirely how much oil there is versus how much is being removed. Another factor is the high cost of fracking. Fracking is used in rock formations where the oil does not flow freely, which means the wells are quickly exhausted compared to conventional wells. A fracked well may initially produce 1,000 barrels a day but then drop off to 100 barrels a day within a few years.

Bakken oil that doesn't move by pipeline is transported by rail.

As domestic production of oil has increased because of fracking, oil prices have dropped from approximately $100/barrel as the 2010s began to less than $60/barrel in 2015.[8] Because of this, the income earned in the lifetime of a fracking well is lower than that earned by a traditional well for two reasons: the well doesn't operate for as many years, and the oil can no longer be sold for as much per barrel.

The final factor is how much of the oil remaining in the Bakken formation is too dispersed to access even with fracking. Deeply buried shale has what is known as diffuse hydrocarbons, meaning that only a small amount of oil is present in a large amount of stone. At the current rate of extraction, scientists with the US Energy Information Agency estimate US production will plateau after 2020.

NONRENEWABLE ENERGY

Energy sources that do not replenish in a short period of time are considered nonrenewable. The four primary nonrenewable energy sources are oil, natural gas, coal, and uranium. Fossil fuels formed from the buried remains of plants and animals that lived millions of years ago and include natural gas, oil, and coal. Uranium ore, used to fuel nuclear power plants, is the only form of nonrenewable energy that is not a fossil fuel.

GLOBAL WARMING

In addition to the dollar value of a barrel of oil, scientists are weighing the price of using the oil in terms of Earth's environment. As of April 2017, the proportion of carbon dioxide in the atmosphere had risen to 410.28 parts per million, the highest level it has ever reached in 650,000 years.[9] Carbon dioxide is an important greenhouse gas. This means it traps heat in the atmosphere. It is released through human activities such as cutting down and burning trees and burning fossil fuels like the gasoline derived from oil. Natural activities including volcanic eruptions also increase the amount of carbon dioxide, but they do not explain the rate increase in the last 50 years.

Because of the increased levels of carbon dioxide and other greenhouse gases, the global temperature has risen 1.7 degrees Fahrenheit (0.9°C) since 1880. In fact, 16 of the 17 warmest years on record have occurred since 2001, with 2016 the warmest year ever recorded.[10] Rising global temperatures affect local environments, making it difficult for certain animals and plants, including crops that people eat, to thrive. Rising temperatures have also melted the ice

"THE MOST IMPORTANT THING ABOUT GLOBAL WARMING IS THIS. WHETHER HUMANS ARE RESPONSIBLE FOR THE BULK OF CLIMATE CHANGE IS GOING TO BE LEFT TO THE SCIENTISTS, BUT IT'S ALL OF OUR RESPONSIBILITY TO LEAVE THIS PLANET IN BETTER SHAPE FOR THE FUTURE GENERATIONS THAN WE FOUND IT."[12]

—MIKE HUCKABEE, FORMER GOVERNOR OF ARKANSAS

caps and glaciers to the point that the amount of naturally occurring ice on the planet is at an all-time low. Sea levels are on the rise, and coastal cities flood more often than ever before.

The effects of global warming are serious enough that nations worldwide are working together under the Paris Agreement, a UN effort to bring world nations together to better understand and address climate change and the various factors that contribute to it. The central feature of this agreement is an effort to reduce climate change as much as possible by preventing a rise in average worldwide temperatures of more than 3.6 degrees Fahrenheit (2°C) and, if possible, to limit this increase to 2.7 degrees Fahrenheit (1.5°C).[11] As of spring 2017, a total of 147 countries, including the United States, have formally agreed to comply with the Paris Agreement. While President Trump signaled in June 2017 that he would withdraw the United States from the agreement, the process to get out will take several years. In the meantime, many US states and companies are continuing to comply.

One concern with DAPL is that it is scheduled to carry enough oil to market that the extraction, processing, transportation, and burning of this fuel will release 111.8 million short tons (101.4 million metric tons) of carbon dioxide into the atmosphere each year. This is the same amount of carbon dioxide that would be released by 21.4 million cars.[13] If the United States burns all of the fossil fuels currently available through existing mines, oil wells, and gas fields, the country will release enough carbon dioxide to take the world 25 percent of the way to a 2.7 degrees Fahrenheit (1.5°C) rise in global temperature, expending 40 percent of the global carbon budget.[14] This would make staying below the agreed threshold much more difficult.

GO GREEN

Limiting global warming will require reducing energy use as well as a shift to renewable sources. Renewable energy, also known as green energy, is generated from a

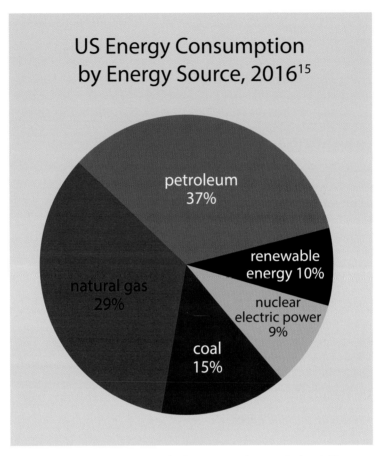

US Energy Consumption
by Energy Source, 2016[15]

petroleum
37%

renewable
energy 10%

natural gas
29%

nuclear
electric power
9%

coal
15%

Petroleum and natural gas supplied approximately two-thirds of US energy
in 2016.

natural source that cannot be depleted, such as the wind

and sun. Supporters of the oil industry worry that a move

toward green energy will mean lost jobs in the oil industry.

Green energy supporters understand that concern and

emphasize that the change will be gradual. They point

out that if no new wells are added and old wells are

allowed to play out, this means the nation will be using 50 percent less oil by 2033.[16] This gives the country 17 years to develop green energy sources and increase the use of green energy. Jobs will be lost in the petroleum industry, but the new industries will need workers.

Historian Jeremy Brecher thinks the transition is possible and cites the US war effort during World War II (1939–1945) as an example. "We need an emergency response like the mobilization of the 1940s," he said.[17] Programs need to be put into place to help communities and specific groups of workers, such as pipe fitters and coal miners, transition from one field to another. But while politicians discuss the need to put programs into place, few have taken the steps to do so. Many politicians continue to focus on increasing domestic oil production.

"IF WE HAVE ANY HOPE OF AVOIDING THE WORST CONSEQUENCES OF CLIMATE CHANGE, WE SHOULD NOT BE BUILDING NEW OIL PIPELINES THAT LOCK US INTO BURNING FOSSIL FUELS FOR GENERATIONS TO COME."[18]

—US SENATOR BERNIE SANDERS

CHAPTER SEVEN

NO SINGLE
PLAN

As the Standing Rock protests continued through 2016, people on both sides of the issue called on the president to intervene. An online petition titled "Tell President Obama: Stop the Dakota Access oil pipeline" collected more than 419,000 signatures.[1] Meanwhile, a September 3, 2016, letter from labor unions representing engineers, laborers, plumbers, electricians, and teamsters called on Obama to approve the easement that would allow the remaining section of the pipeline to be completed.

Protesters gathered outside the White House in September 2016, during President Obama's administration.

On October 31, 2016, a Facebook post stated that law enforcement was targeting protesters through their Facebook location. Facebook users from around the world began checking in, giving their location as Standing Rock. Although police denied this claim, by November 1, 2016, the number of check-ins had reached 1.5 million.[2] Whether or not the post was true, these people stood in support of Standing Rock.

Military veterans had also noted the use of police and security forces equipped as military. Some of these veterans formed Veterans Stand for Standing Rock, and 2,000 of them had traveled to Standing Rock by December 3.[3] Peaceful and unarmed, they joined with protesters. Marine veteran Jade Emilio Snell explained he wasn't against the pipeline project but found the treatment of protesters unacceptable. "I've been watching the news, how they're spraying everybody and using rubber bullets, and these guys are fighting for what they believe in and as a veteran we took an oath," he said. "We're not just there to protect Americans in foreign countries. We're here to protect this country inside of it, too."[4]

The Veterans for Standing Rock group sought to protect the protesters' First Amendment rights to free speech and assembly.

On December 4, 2016, Obama asked the USACE to review the permit that had been approved so that the pipeline could cross the Missouri River, specifically checking the route and looking to see if an alternate path was possible. Speaking later, Obama said, "As a general rule, my view is that there is a way for us to accommodate sacred lands of Native Americans. And I think, right now, that the Army Corps is examining whether there are ways to reroute this pipeline."[5]

NO BIG PICTURE

Because the building of a pipeline is largely a matter of state and local jurisdiction, ETP had to get numerous permits, easements, and licenses. There were also meetings with city governments, town residents, reservation leaders, and businesses of various kinds. Each group considered its own interests, such as whether the pipeline would bring tax money to the area or whether it could possibly pollute the drinking water. Even if these groups knew the USACE had to do an environmental impact statement, people assumed

PERMISSION BY THE NUMBERS

Because no single governmental body oversees pipelines, ETP had to deal with many different state and local governments as well as cities and reservations. The pipeline runs through four states—North and South Dakota, Iowa, and Illinois. Although it doesn't cross any reservation, it crosses near and could potentially impact four—Fort Berthold in North Dakota, Standing Rock in North and South Dakota, the Cheyenne River Reservation in South Dakota, and the Lake Traverse Reservation in South Dakota. Pipelines don't customarily go through cities, but cities within 20 miles (32 km) of the pipeline include Bismarck, North Dakota; Sioux Falls, South Dakota; Des Moines, Iowa; and Jacksonville, Illinois.

it must have been done competently because a permit was issued.

What they didn't consider was how damaging such assumptions could be, especially when the topic is environmental impact. "Water systems are complicated and messy," explained Jennifer Veilleux.[6] When the USACE allowed construction to proceed based on the requirements for a Nationwide Permit No. 12, the agency may have considered the environment right where the pipe is being laid but paid no attention to the larger environment of the lake, river, or surrounding watershed.

This oversight could be critical, according to findings by the US Department of Transportation's Pipeline and Hazardous Materials Safety Administration (PHMSA). The agency reported that pipelines that cross rivers

WATERSHED REALITY

A watershed is an area of land that drains into a single body of water. The Standing Rock Reservation is in the Missouri River watershed. So are the cities of Omaha in Nebraska, Kansas City in Kansas and Missouri, and even Jefferson City, the capital of Missouri. A watershed is like a funnel, and the water it gathers is channeled through the soil and into creeks and streams and into larger rivers. Watersheds don't always stop at state or national borders. When a river forms the border between two states, such as the Columbia River between Oregon and Washington or the Mississippi River between Texas and Louisiana, the watershed extends into both states. What happens in one part of the watershed can affect the environment, the economy, and the health of the entire area.

"BISMARCK RESIDENTS DON'T WANT THEIR WATER THREATENED, SO WHY IS IT OK FOR NORTH DAKOTA TO REACT WITH GUNS AND TANKS WHEN NATIVE AMERICANS ASK FOR THE SAME RIGHT?"[7]

—REVEREND JESSE JACKSON, CIVIL RIGHTS ACTIVIST

and streams, whether in the streambed, through the water, or above the water, pose a much higher risk to the environment than pipelines confined to land. According to the PHMSA, the proximity to water increases the danger due to several factors, including the risk of flooding, change in the speed of water flow, and changes in the river or stream bank. Any of these things is enough to cause the stream or river to cut a new channel for itself and undermine the soil supporting the pipeline, which can change pressure on the pipeline or expose the pipeline to debris. Either of these issues could cause a rupture. None of these possibilities are examined in the report because the USACE doesn't consider the river as a whole, only the small portion crossed by the pipeline.

RED VS. BLUE

The pipeline didn't just highlight the boundaries between states, cities, and reservations. It also provided a microcosm of politics in the United States at the time of

A number of celebrities spoke against DAPL, including actress Shailene Woodley, *second from right*, who traveled to the Standing Rock camp and was arrested during a protest.

the 2016 presidential election, as the nation divided along party lines. Opinions about the pipeline were often linked to the stance voters took on a variety of issues, including civil rights and energy. Voters and the media grew increasingly outspoken until it seemed as if no middle ground remained.

With Democrats often serving as advocates for both the environment and civil rights, the most visible high-level Democrat to take a stance in support of the water protesters was Vermont senator Bernie Sanders, who had run for president as a Democrat but lost the nomination to former secretary of state Hillary Clinton in the spring of 2016. The senator called on Obama to halt construction, and when the president did so, Sanders supported his decision. Sanders said,

> I appreciate very much President Obama listening to the Native American people. . . . In the year 2016, we should not continue to trample on Native American sovereignty. We should not endanger the water supply of millions of people. We should not become more dependent on fossil fuel and accelerate the planetary crisis of climate change. Our job now is to transform our energy system away from fossil fuels, not to produce more greenhouse gas emissions.[8]

Sanders also participated in a number of protests against DAPL, including a November 15, 2016, protest outside the White House just a week after the presidential election.

Before the election, voters questioned why Trump and Clinton remained quiet on

PRESIDENTIAL MEMORANDUM

On January 24, 2017, just four days after taking office, President Trump signed a memorandum telling the secretary of the army to instruct his subordinates to "review and approve in an expedited manner" the approvals needed to finish constructing the pipeline.[9] It is worth noting that presidents do not ordinarily have legal authority to just ignore the law. Trump could not simply approve the pipeline himself in violation of the Clean Water Act, the National Environmental Policy Act, and other federal laws. But he can let the US Army know his stance, as he did with this memo. Following this memo, the USACE decided a complete review was not necessary after all, as Obama had previously requested, and it approved the permit.

DAPL. Political analysts pointed out that Clinton was most likely caught between two key groups of political allies— Native American activists and environmentalists on one side and the labor unions that often support Democrats on the other.

Although Trump did not speak out before the election, the financial disclosure forms he filed show he was an investor in ETP. Trump's investment in the company was somewhere between $500,000 and $1 million. The money goes both ways: ETP's chief executive, Kelcy Warren, donated $103,000 to Trump's campaign fund prior to Trump's Republican primary win and another $66,800 to the Republican National Committee after.[10] Days after his inauguration, Trump published a memo demanding the completion of the pipeline.

"THE DAKOTA ACCESS PIPELINE (DAPL) UNDER DEVELOPMENT BY DAKOTA ACCESS, LLC, REPRESENTS A SUBSTANTIAL, MULTI-BILLION-DOLLAR PRIVATE INVESTMENT IN OUR NATION'S ENERGY INFRASTRUCTURE. . . . I BELIEVE THAT CONSTRUCTION AND OPERATION OF LAWFULLY PERMITTED PIPELINE INFRASTRUCTURE SERVES THE NATIONAL INTEREST."[11]

—PRESIDENT DONALD TRUMP, PRESIDENTIAL MEMORANDUM REGARDING CONSTRUCTION OF THE DAKOTA ACCESS PIPELINE, JANUARY 24, 2017

FROM THE HEADLINES

WINNING THE FIGHT

Recent news stories might suggest the USACE takes the side of big business over environmental concerns and Native American tribes, but that isn't always so. In 2015, the Lummi Nation, which lives north of Seattle, Washington, filed a petition with the USACE to stop the Gateway Pacific Terminal. Members claimed the terminal would damage sacred sites and their traditional fishing area. Their right to fish in this area had been guaranteed by an 1855 treaty. The planned terminal would have been built on land held by the Crow Nation, but the USACE said that it had to comply with the treaty rights of the Lummi and denied the permits needed to construct the transportation terminal.

The Lummi aren't the only Native American victors. The Quinault Indian Nation, which has fishing rights in Grays Harbor southwest of Seattle, Washington, challenged the construction of an oil transportation terminal. The station would have received up to 17.8 million barrels of oil each year, including Bakken crude.[12] Tribe members said expanding the existing station would endanger their fishing rights and the surrounding ocean environment. In January 2017, the Washington Supreme Court, which heard the case, agreed that the Ocean Resources Management Act covers onshore development that puts aquatic resources at risk. This move by the state supreme court reversed decisions by both a state board and the state court of appeals.

Members of several Northwest Coast Native Nations, including the Lummi, unveil a totem pole celebrating unity among US and Canadian tribes in opposing oil pipeline expansion.

CHAPTER EIGHT

DAPL AND
THE FUTURE

After the water protectors had weathered harsh winter conditions, North Dakota Governor Doug Burgum ordered them to evacuate the camps by February 23, 2017. Most protesters complied, some of them walking across the frozen river onto the Standing Rock Reservation. Burgum ordered the evacuation because of annual spring floods along the river. He wanted to give workers time to clear out the trash and human waste that protesters left behind to keep it from polluting the river during a flood. Tom Goldtooth, executive director of the Indigenous Environmental Network, disagrees with the governor's reason for ordering the evacuation. He called it an infringement on the water protectors' right to protest and freedom of

Members of law enforcement and the National Guard made the last Standing Rock protestors move out of their camp.

speech. He added that the protectors have not given up. Several court cases still need to be heard.

LEGAL BATTLES AND LEAKS

Oil began flowing through the pipeline starting in May 2017. But it takes several weeks to fill a pipeline with oil, and before the pipeline was fully operational, three oil leaks had already been reported earlier that spring. On March 3, 2017, near Waterford City, North Dakota, two barrels of oil seeped out from a leaky flange, the point where two pipes are joined. The oil flow was immediately stopped, the spill was contained, and soil and snow were removed as needed. On March 5, in a rural section of Mercer County, North Dakota, another half barrel of oil leaked aboveground. This time the problem was valve failure, and oil flow was stopped so that the valve could be replaced. Officials say no waterways were affected. In April, another two barrels leaked in Spink Country, South Dakota. A leaky pump was to blame, and the oil was cleaned up using absorbent materials and returned to the pipe.

These and other spills are why the lawsuits pending against ETP are so important, says Dave Archambault II, a

MORE TO THE
STORY

DAPL IN COURT

The Standing Rock tribe was not the only group to go to court to try to stop DAPL. In September 2016, the Yankton Sioux Tribe filed a lawsuit against the USACE and the US Fish and Wildlife Service for allowing pipeline construction without a full environmental impact statement. They said the construction violated the Clean Water Act, the National Environmental Policy Act, and the National Historic Preservation Act. They also called for additional talks with the people of Standing Rock as described in the UN Declaration of the Rights of Indigenous People. "The United Nations Declaration reflects what all Native people understand, that our complete world view is based on relationship—relationship with the land, water, and all living things dictates how we conduct ourselves on Mother Earth," said Faith Spotted Eagle, chair for the Ihanktonwan Treaty Steering Committee. The Yankton Sioux call themselves the Ihanktonwan Oyate. Said Spotted Eagle, "Those in power only have relationship with themselves and their sources of power; in this case, how much money they can make. It is a sad state of affairs, but we will persevere. I pray for those who destroy sacred sites as there are consequences in the natural world."[1]

Standing Rock leader. "This is foreboding as the company does not yet have a plan in place to address how they would contain and clean a serious spill," he said. "We will continue to battle the operation of this pipeline in court and remind everyone that just because the oil is flowing now doesn't mean that it can't be stopped."[2] Earthjustice, a nonprofit organization that specializes in environmental law, began handling the Standing Rock lawsuit.

SLOW DOWNS

With multiple points where a law or policy could be vetoed or a case could be appealed, environmental groups are always looking for more effective ways to make oil and other fossil fuel companies listen. They sometimes make themselves heard by finding ways to cost these big companies money. Although protesters did not permanently halt DAPL, ETP was not able to fulfill the original contract as negotiated, which required having oil flowing by the beginning of 2017. This means they had to negotiate a new contract at a time when oil prices were lower. Since prices have dropped from $70 to $80

Protesters in Utah call for Wells Fargo bank and others to stop investing in DAPL and other pipelines, another economic strategy to slow down oil companies.

per barrel to $40 to $50 per barrel, at the rate of 450,000 to 570,000 barrels per day, this cost the company millions of dollars per day.[3] The protesters may not have halted the pipeline, but they did cost the company money. The belief is that if they cost a company enough money, the company may decide to take their concerns more seriously in the future because ignoring environmental concerns has already been an expensive mistake.

Native American groups also have the power to slow down oil companies because they are able to call treaty rights into play. When various tribes signed treaties with the US Government, they gave their lands, or portions thereof, to the government. In return, they received the right to hunt, fish, and gather on the lands reserved for them or within other recognized territories that they had handed over. They have these rights in perpetuity, or forever. If a pipeline crosses treaty land or may affect lands that Native Americans have the right to use because of a treaty, the group threatening the tribal use of the land might be in violation of a treaty. This means the tribe in question can take the other group to court, as the Standing Rock and Cheyenne River Sioux tribes did when they took ETP to a federal court in early February 2017. In the lawsuit, the tribes said that the company threatened not only their drinking water but also their right to practice their religion. A federal judge denied their claim, but the two tribes had managed, yet again, to threaten the completion and operation of the pipeline. In this way, tribal rights offer one more opportunity to put a halt to or at least create a costly delay for a project like a pipeline.

In June 2017, a judge ordered the USACE to reevaluate its environmental review of the pipeline, saying the USACE did not consider the effects of the pipeline on the hunting and fishing rights of the Standing Rock Sioux. The decision did not immediately halt the oil in the pipeline while the USACE studies its review.

The tribe of Standing Rock and the protesters weren't

I OBJECT

The Standing Rock protests weren't the only ones that took place along the route of DAPL, although they were the only ones that made the national news. In early November 2016, protesters set up a camp to block construction near where the pipeline would cross the Des Moines River. During the early morning on November 10, three of these protesters climbed into the pipe itself. When workers arrived, they couldn't reach the protesters, who had taken their positions approximately 50 feet (15 m) from the opening. The workers tried banging on the pipe, but the protesters did not leave until they were dragged out by police.

able to halt the oil permanently, but they did cost ETP money. They gathered together supporters from many reservations, from all over the nation, and from around the world. For many Native Americans, this show of support is a good sign. As Chanse Adams-Zavalla, a former resident of Maidu Reservation in California, explains, "This isn't the *end* of our movement. It's the beginning. . . . Even if somehow, someway, they build this pipeline, they've inadvertently sparked a whole generation of us indigenous folks and everyone who wants to stand with us to fight for Mother Earth. We're going to inherit this planet, bro, and everyone's welcome to inherit it with us if they want."[4]

The support and the news coverage showed many that indigenous rights and environmental concerns aren't just something that matters along the Missouri River. They

"SOMETIMES PEOPLE JUST SAY, LIKE, THEY'RE OPPOSED TO PIPELINE DEVELOPMENT, AND THEY'RE OPPOSED TO PIPELINES. WELL, THAT'S FINE, AND THEY'RE ENTITLED TO THEIR OPINION, BUT PIPELINE DEVELOPMENT IS LEGALLY PERMISSIBLE IN NORTH DAKOTA, AND WE'RE OBLIGATED TO ENFORCE THE LAWS. SO WHEN A COMPANY MEETS THE CONDITIONS SET BY LAW FOR A PERMIT, THEY RECEIVE ONE."[5]

—JULIE FEDORCHAK, NORTH DAKOTA PUBLIC SERVICE COMMISSIONER

The water protectors braved harsh conditions to stand up for what they believed in.

aren't just a US concern. They are of global interest and attract attention worldwide even when they start locally, with a group of Native Americans standing up for what they believe.

ESSENTIAL
FACTS

MAJOR EVENTS

- Lakota residents of Standing Rock Reservation were angry their objections over the route of the Dakota Access Pipeline (DAPL) had been ignored. Starting in April 2016, several camps were set up, and water protectors gathered to pray and protest. As social media spread the story, thousands of people, both Native Americans and environmentalists, joined the camps and the protests.

- On December 4, 2016, President Barack Obama requested that the US Army Corps of Engineers (USACE) do a full environmental study. The USACE denied the right-of-way the pipeline developer, Energy Transfer Partners (ETP), needed.

- On January 24, 2017, President Donald Trump issued a memorandum requesting the completion of DAPL.

KEY PLAYERS

- ETP designed and built DAPL.

- Members of Standing Rock Reservation objected to DAPL because it crosses the Missouri River near where the reservation draws its water.

- The USACE approved the permit ETP needed to build the final section of the pipeline over the Missouri River.

IMPACT ON SOCIETY

The protests surrounding DAPL mirrored the divisions running deep through US society—Republican versus Democrat, oil companies versus environmentalists. It also spurred discussions about how institutional racism factors into the way indigenous rights are handled in the United States.

QUOTE

"This movement isn't just about our reservation—it's about speaking up when you feel that something is wrong."

—*Tokata Iron Eyes, Standing Rock Reservation resident, age 12*

GLOSSARY

CIVILIAN

Not serving in the armed forces.

CONFEDERACY

An alliance of people or groups.

CONFLUENCE

The place where two rivers join and become one.

CORRODE

To slowly eat or wear away.

EASEMENT

The right of a nonowner to access or use someone's land for a specific purpose.

FRACKING

The process of forcing water into oil shafts to break the rock and release the oil.

HYDROCARBONS

Organic molecules, such as oil and oil products, that contain hydrogen atoms and carbon atoms.

INDIGENOUS PEOPLE

People who identify with a certain area and are descended from people who lived there before modern government.

JURISDICTION

The power to make legal decisions.

PETROLEUM

Also known as crude oil, this fossil fuel can be processed into heating oil or gasoline.

WATERSHED

The area of land that drains into a given body of water, such as a river or gulf.

ADDITIONAL
RESOURCES

SELECTED BIBLIOGRAPHY

Abidor, Jen. "I Led a Movement to Protect My Land."
    Seventeen. Mar.–Apr. 2017: 24. Print.

Josephy, Alvin M. *500 Nations*. New York: Knopf, 1994. Print.

Rolo, Mark Anthony. "The Indian Wars Have Never Ended."
    Progressive. Feb. 2017: 35–36. Print.

FURTHER READINGS

Marsico, Katie. *Indigenous People's Rights*. Minneapolis, MN:
    Abdo, 2011. Print.

McLaughlin, Timothy P., editor. *Walking on Earth & Touching
    the Sky: Poetry and Prose by Lakota Youth at Red Cloud
    Indian School*. New York: Abrams, 2012. Print.

ONLINE RESOURCES

To learn more about the Dakota Access Pipeline, visit **abdobooklinks.com**. These links are routinely monitored and updated to provide the most current information available.

MORE INFORMATION

For more information on this subject, contact or visit the following organizations:

Standing Rock Sioux Tribe
P.O. Box D
Fort Yates, ND 58538
701-854-8500
standingrock.org
The website for the reservation includes information on the group's history, recent news updates, and information on the Dakota Access Pipeline.

United States Army Corp of Engineers
441 G Street NW
Washington, DC 20314-1000
202-761-0011
usace.army.mil
Contact the USACE for information on DAPL and other projects or recreation opportunities on public lands.

SOURCE NOTES

CHAPTER 1. YOUTH LEADING THE WAY

1. "Rezpect Our Water: Sign Our Petition." *Rezpect Our Water*. YouTube, 27 Apr. 2016. Web. 19 July 2017.

2. Alan Taylor. "The Exxon Valdez Oil Spill: 25 Years Ago Today." *Atlantic*. Atlantic Monthly Group, 24 Mar. 2014. Web. 19 July 2017.

3. "Rezpect Our Water: Sign Our Petition." *Rezpect Our Water*. YouTube, 27 Apr. 2016. Web. 19 July 2017.

4. Mallory Black. "Indian Country Unites to Block Dakota Access Pipeline." *Native Peoples* 1 Nov. 2016: 14. Print.

5. Jen Abidor. "I Led a Movement to Protect My Land." *Seventeen* Mar.–Apr. 2017: 24. Print.

6. Wes Enzinna. "Crude Awakening." *Mother Jones* Jan.–Feb. 2017: 36. Print.

7. Jen Abidor. "I Led a Movement to Protect My Land." *Seventeen* Mar.–Apr. 2017: 24. Print.

8. Tyler Parry. "Man's Best Friend." *History Today* Dec. 2016: 51. Print.

9. Nathan Rott and Eyder Peralta. "In Victory for Protesters, Army Halts Construction of Dakota Pipeline." *The Two-Way*. NPR, 4 Dec. 2016. Web. 19 July 2017.

10. "Rezpect Our Water: Sign Our Petition." *Rezpect Our Water*. YouTube, 27 Apr. 2016. Web. 19 July 2017.

11. "Pipeline Protests Cloud Future for Native Americans." *Pipeline and Gas Journal* Feb. 2017: 80. Print.

12. Ibid. 67.

13. Jo Miles and Hugh MacMillan. "Who's Banking on the Dakota Access Pipeline?" *Food & Water Watch*. Food & Water Watch, 6 Sept. 2016. Web. 19 July 2017.

14. Nika Knight. "Call for DOJ Observers in North Dakota as DAPL Activists Face Severe Injuries, Arrests." *Counter Current News*. Counter Current News, 24 Nov. 2016. Web. 19 July 2017.

CHAPTER 2. BUILDING DAPL

1. "About." *Dakota Access: Pipeline Facts*. DAPLPipelineFacts, 2017. Web. 19 July 2017.

2. "Where Are Liquids Pipelines Located?" *Pipeline 101*. Pipeline101.org, 2016. Web. 19 July 2017.

3. "How Much Water Does the Typical Hydraulically Fractured Well Require?" *USGS*. US Geological Survey, 21 June 2017. Web. 19 July 2017.

4. Jennifer Oldman, et al. "Boom and Bust in the Bakken Oil Fields." *Bloomberg*. Bloomberg, 29 Nov. 2015. Web. 19 July 2017.

5. Noreen O'Donnell. "Thousands of New Pipeline Jobs? Those Are Temporary." *NBC Miami*. NBC Universal Media, 24 Jan. 2017. Web. 19 July 2017.

6. Richard Nemec. "Dakota Access Pipeline: A New Artery for Bakken Crude." *Pipeline and Gas Journal* Aug. 2016: 16–17. Print.

7. Nick Stockton. "The Dismal Science of the Standing Rock Pipeline Protests." *Wired*. Condé Nast, 3 Nov. 2016. Web. 19 July 2017.

8. Richard Nemec. "Dakota Access Pipeline: A New Artery for Bakken Crude." *Pipeline and Gas Journal* Aug. 2016: 16–17. Print.

9. "Dakota Access Pipeline: Top 3 Pros and Cons." *ProCon*. ProCon, 23 Nov. 2016. Web. 19 July 2017.

10. "Safety." *Dakota Access: Pipeline Facts*. DAPLPipelineFacts, 2017. Web. 19 July 2017.

11. Gwen Ifill. "Why North Dakota's Oil Fields Are So Deadly for Workers" *PBS Newshour*. NewsHour Productions, 24 June 2015. Web. 19 July 2017.

12. Jennifer Gollan. "Oil Field Workers Keep Dying, and the Feds Want to Know Why." *Mother Jones*. Mother Jones, 24 Aug. 2015. Web. 19 July 2017.

13. Ron Meador. "Suppressed Memo Shows Many Failings in Corps Review of Dakota Access Plan." *MinnPost*. MinnPost, 3 Mar. 2017. Web. 19 July 2017.

14. "Enbridge Estimates Oil Spill Cleanup at $1.2 Billion." *Wood TV*. Nexstar Broadcasting, 3 Nov. 2014. Web. 19 July 2017.

15. Hari Sreenivasan. "CEO behind Dakota Access to Protesters: 'We're Building the Pipeline.'" *PBS Newshour*. NewsHour Productions, 16 Nov. 2016. Web. 3 Apr. 2017.

CHAPTER 3. RESERVATION LANDS

1. Amy Corbin. "Black Hills." *Sacred Land Film Project*. Earth Island Institute, 1 Nov. 2003. Web. 19 July 2017.

2. "May 22, 1843: A Thousand Pioneers Head West on the Oregon Trail." *History*. A&E Television Networks, 2017. Web. 19 July 2017.

3. Todd Underwood. "The Oregon Trail." *Frontier Trails of the Old West*. atJeu Publishing, 2000. Web. 19 July 2017.

4. Alvin M Josephy. *500 Nations*. New York: Knopf, 1994. Print. 397.

5. "American Bison: Almost Extinct." *Smithsonian*. Smithsonian Institution, 2014. Web. 19 July 2017.

6. J. Weston Phippen. "Kill Every Buffalo You Can! Every Buffalo Dead Is an Indian Gone." *Atlantic*. Atlantic Monthly Group, 13 May 2016. Web. 19 July 2017.

7. Dee Brown. *Bury My Heart at Wounded Knee: An Indian History of the American West*. New York: Sterling, 2009. *Google Book Search*. Web. 19 July 2017.

8. Alvin M Josephy. *500 Nations*. New York: Alfred A. Knopf, 1994. Print. 398–402.

9. "Breakup of the Great Sioux Reservation." *North Dakota Studies*. State Historical Society of North Dakota, n.d. Web. 19 July 2017.

10. Ibid.

11. Alvin M Josephy. *500 Nations*. New York: Alfred A. Knopf, 1994. Print. 398.

12. "Indian Boarding Schools." *US-Dakota War of 1862*. Minnesota Historical Society, n.d. Web. 19 July 2017.

CHAPTER 4. INDIGENOUS RIGHTS

1. "Frequently Asked Questions." *Indian Affairs*. US Department of the Interior, 17 July 2017. Web. 19 July 2017.

2. Valerie Volcovici. "Trump Advisors Aim to Privatize Oil-Rich Indian Reservations." *Reuters*. Reuters, 5 Dec. 2016. Web. 19 July 2017.

3. Ibid.

4. Wes Enzinna. "Crude Awakening." *Mother Jones* Jan.–Feb. 2017: 36. Print.

5. Ron Johnson. "Nations Rising." *Earth Island Journal* Winter 2017: 18–26. Print.

SOURCE NOTES
CONTINUED

CHAPTER 5. WATER SAFETY

1. Ernest Scheyder. "For Standing Rock Sioux, New Water System May Reduce Oil Leak Risk." *Reuters*. Reuters, 22 Nov. 2016. Web. 19 July 2017.

2. Rebecca Hersher. "Canadian Oil Spill Threatens Drinking Water." *The Two-Way*. NPR. 25 July 2016. Web. 19 July 2017.

3. Tiffany Stecker. "Will the Pipeline Fight Affect Future Permitting?" *E&E News*. Environment & Energy Publishing, 3 Nov. 2016. Web. 19 July 2017.

4. "How Much Water Does the Typical Hydraulically Fractured Well Require?" *USGS*. US Geological Survey, 21 June 2017. Web. 19 July 2017.

5. "Clean Up Underway for Nearly 3M-Gallon Saltwater Spill in ND." *Rapid City Journal*. Rapid City Journal, 22 Jan. 2015. Web. 19 July 2017.

6. Talli Nauman. "Contamination of Fresh Water 'Very Serious Environmental Threat.'" *Native Sun News*. Dakota Resource Council, 20 Mar. 2015. Web. 19 July 2017.

CHAPTER 6. THE PRICE OF OIL

1. "Americans Use Many Types of Energy." *US Energy Information Administration*. US Department of Energy, 19 May 2017. Web. 19 July 2017.

2. "An America First Energy Plan." *White House*. White House, n.d. Web. 19 July 2017.

3. "Dakota Access Pipeline: Top 3 Pros and Cons." *ProCon*. ProCon, 23 Nov. 2016. Web. 19 July 2017.

4. Lucia Mutikani. "Oil Imports Lift US Trade Deficit to Near Five-Year High." *Reuters*. Reuters, 7 Mar. 2017. Web. 19 July 2017.

5. Vera Bergengruen. "Trump May Doubt Climate Change, Pentagon Sees It as Threat Multiplier." *Military.com*. Military Advantage, 2 June 2017. Web. 19 July 2017.

6. "Dakota Access Pipeline: Top 3 Pros and Cons." *ProCon*. ProCon, 23 Nov. 2016. Web. 19 July 2017.

7. "How Much Oil and Gas Are Actually in the Bakken Formation?" *USGS*. US Geological Society, 21 June 2017. Web. 19 July 2017.

8. Dennis Dimick. "How Long Can the U.S. Oil Boom Last?" *National Geographic*. National Geographic Partners, 19 Dec. 2014. Web. 19 July 2017.

9. "Global Climate Change: Vital Signs of the Planet." *Global Climate Change*. NASA, 17 July 2017. Web. 19 July 2017.

10. Ibid.

11. "The Paris Agreement." *UNFCCC*. United Nations Framework Convention on Climate Change, 2014. Web. 19 July 2017.

12. "California Republican Debate Transcript." *NBC News*. NBC News, 4 May 2007. Web. 19 July 2017.

13. "Dakota Access Pipeline: Top 3 Pros and Cons." *ProCon*. ProCon, 23 Nov. 2016. Web. 19 July 2017.

14. Bill McKibbon. "Recalculating the Climate Math." *New Republic* Nov. 2016: 16-17. Print.

15. "Americans Use Many Types of Energy." *US Energy Information Administration*. US Department of Energy, 19 May 2017. Web. 19 July 2017.

16. Bill McKibbon. "Recalculating the Climate Math." *New Republic* Nov. 2016: 17. Print.

17. Jon Queally. "Amid Tribal Pipeline Fight, Internal AFL-CIO Letter Exposes 'Very Real Split.'" *National Nurse* July–Sept. 2016: 21. Print.

18. "Dakota Access Pipeline: Top 3 Pros and Cons." *ProCon*. ProCon, 23 Nov. 2016. Web. 19 July 2017.

CHAPTER 7. NO SINGLE PLAN

1. "Tell President Obama: Stop the Dakota Access Oil Pipeline." *Credo Action*. Credo Action, n.d. Web. 19 July 2017.

2. Merrit Kennedy. "More Than 1 Million 'Check-In' on Facebook to Support the Standing Rock Sioux." *The Two-Way*. NPR, 1 Nov. 2016. Web. 19 July 2017.

3. Ryan W. Miller. "How the Dakota Access Pipeline Battle Unfolded." *USA Today*. USA Today, 4 Dec. 2016. Web. 19 July 2017.

4. Sophie Lewis. "Veterans Unite for Second 'Deployment' Against Dakota Access Pipeline." *CNN*. CNN, 9 Feb. 2017. Web. 19 July 2017.

5. Weston Williams. "Obama Expresses Support for Native Americans in Pipeline Clash." *Christian Science Monitor*. Christian Science Monitor, 3 Nov. 2016. Web. 19 July 2017.

6. Jennifer Veilleux. Personal Interview. 14 Mar. 2017.

7. Aaron P Bernstein. "Jesse Jackson Joins Pipeline Protest Effort; FAA Issues 'No-Fly' Restriction." *Bismarck Tribune*. Bismarck Tribune, 26 Oct. 2016. Web. 19 July 2017.

8. "Sanders Statement on Dakota Access Pipeline Decision." *Bernie Sanders: US Senator for Vermont*. Bernie Sanders, 4 Dec. 2016. Web. 19 July 2017.

9. Donald J. Trump. "Presidential Memorandum Regarding Construction of the Dakota Access Pipeline." *The White House*. The White House, 24 Jan. 2017. Web. 19 July 2017.

10. Oliver Milman. "Dakota Access Pipeline Company and Donald Trump Have Close Financial Ties." *Guardian*. Guardian News, 26 Oct. 2016. Web. 19 July 2017.

11. Donald J. Trump. "Presidential Memorandum Regarding Construction of the Dakota Access Pipeline." *The White House*. The White House, 24 Jan. 2017. Web. 19 July 2017.

12. Lynda V. Mapes. "State Court Rules against Plans for Big Grays Harbor Oil Terminal." *Seattle Times*. Seattle Times Company, 12 Jan. 2017. Web. 19 July 2017.

CHAPTER 8. DAPL AND THE FUTURE

1. "Yankton Sioux Tribe Sues US Army Corps, USFWS Over Dakota Access." *Indian Country Today*. Indian Country Media Network, 9 Sep. 2016. Web. 19 July 2017.

2. "The Standing Rock Sioux Tribes Litigation on the Dakota Access Pipeline." *Earthjustice*. Earthjustice, 17 July 2017. Web. 19 July 2017.

3. Richard Nemec. "Dakota Access Pipeline: A New Artery for Bakken Crude." *Pipeline and Gas Journal* Aug. 2016: 16-17. Print.

4. Wes Enzinna. "Crude Awakening." *Mother Jones* Jan.–Feb. 2017: 37. Print.

5. Hari Sreenivasan. "Despite Protests, Dakota Access Pipeline Nears Completion." *PBS NewsHour*. NewsHour Productions, 26 Feb. 2017. Web. 19 July 2017.

INDEX

American Indian Movement, 40–41
Amnesty International, 16, 45
Army Corps of Engineers (USACE), 7,
    12–13, 60, 61, 63, 81, 82–84, 86,
    88, 93, 97

Bakken oil, 7, 18, 20–21, 23, 25, 26,
    68, 70, 72, 88
Bismarck, North Dakota, 7, 8, 49, 82
Black Hills, 30, 32, 34–36, 41, 50
boarding schools, 39–40
Brave Bull, Ladonna Allard, 9
brine, 64–65
Burgum, Doug, 90
burial grounds, 9, 60

carbon dioxide, 73, 75
Clean Water Act of 1972, 7, 54, 61,
    86, 93
climate change, 69, 73–74, 86
Clinton, Hillary, 85, 86–87
Crazy Horse, 35–36
Custer, George Armstrong, 34–36

Dawes Act of 1887, 47
Declaration on the Rights of
    Indigenous Peoples, 49–51, 93

Earthjustice, 95
Emergency Planning and Community
    Right to Know Act, 55
Enbridge pipeline, 27, 59
Energy Information Agency, US, 72
Energy Transfer Partners (ETP), 6,
    14, 15, 18, 23–24, 26, 49, 56,
    59, 62, 87, 95–96, 98
  lawsuits, 92, 97
  permits, 12, 60, 82
environmental impact, 8, 22, 26,
    27, 52, 54, 55, 64–65, 73–75,
    83–84
  report, 59–63, 82–83, 93, 97
Environmental Protection Agency
    (EPA), 54, 61

Fort Laramie Treaty of 1851, 32, 45
Fort Laramie Treaty of 1868, 33, 37
fossil fuels, 55, 72, 73, 75, 86
fracking, 21–23, 55, 64, 68, 70, 72

Great Sioux Reservation, 33–37, 39

Indian Child Welfare Act, 40
indigenous, 45, 50
Indigenous Environmental Network,
    47, 90
institutional racism, 47–50

job creation, 14, 23, 24, 77

Lake Oahe, 7, 44, 45, 49, 56, 60
Lakota, 6, 28, 30–33, 35, 36, 39,
   41, 50
law enforcement, 11–12, 16, 80, 97

Mahmoud, Joey, 24
Missouri River, 6, 7, 9, 49, 58, 60,
   81, 83

National Environmental Policy Act,
   52, 86, 93
Nationwide Permit No. 12, 12, 60, 61,
   81, 83, 86

Obama, Barack, 60, 70, 78, 81–82,
   86
Oceti Sakowin (Seven Council Fires),
   9, 11
oil dependence, 14, 22, 66, 68, 86
oil prices, 22, 23, 24, 68, 72,
   95–96
oil spills, 8, 27, 56, 58–59, 60,
   62–63, 84, 92, 95
Organization of Petroleum Exporting
   Countries (OPEC), 66

Paris Agreement, 74–75
petroleum, 18, 21–22, 64, 66, 77
Pipeline and Hazardous Materials
   Safety Administration (PHMSA),
   27, 83–84
pipelines, 18, 20, 23, 25–27, 58, 59,
   60, 62, 63, 64–65, 82, 83–84,
   92, 96
privatization, 46–47
protests, 9, 11–12, 15, 16, 78, 80, 85,
   86, 90, 95–96, 97–98
Public Service Commission, 58

renewable energy, 75–77
reservations, 31–34, 35, 36, 37,
   39–41, 42, 44, 45–47, 96–97
Rezpect Our Water, 4, 6, 8

Sacred Circle, 9
safety, 26–27, 49, 56, 59, 64–65,
   84
Sanders, Bernie, 85–86
Silent Spring, 52, 54
Sioux, 6, 11, 15, 28, 30, 32–37
Sioux Bill, 37
social media, 12, 80
Standing Rock Reservation, 6, 7, 12,
   28, 34, 39, 42, 44–45, 49, 80,
   82, 83, 90
   Sioux tribe, 11, 15, 16, 37, 39, 41,
   42, 44–45, 49, 56, 58–59, 93,
   95, 96–97
   sovereignty, 41, 44
   Standing Rock Agency, 33–34
   youth, 4, 6, 8

taxation, 14, 25, 82
trade deficit, 68
Trump, Donald, 46, 66, 68, 70,
   74–75, 86, 87

United Nations (UN), 45, 49–51, 74

Veterans Stand for Standing Rock,
   80

Warren, Kelcy, 87
water protectors, 9, 13–14, 27, 90,
   92
water supply, 6–8, 9, 22, 49, 56,
   58–59, 64–65, 82–83, 86, 97

ABOUT THE
AUTHOR

Sue Bradford Edwards is a Missouri nonfiction author who writes about culture and history, including matters of race. She has written ten books for Abdo Publishing, including *Black Lives Matter*, *Hidden Human Computers*, and *What Are Race and Racism?*.